Language Arts Bingo Book

COMPLETE BINGO GAME IN A BOOK

PARTS OF SPEECH
Noun
Verb
Adjective
Adverb

Written By Rebecca Stark

ISBN 978-0-87386-464-0

Educational Books 'n' Bingo

Printed in the U.S.A.

LANGUAGE ARTS BINGO DIRECTIONS

INCLUDED:

List of Terms

Templates for Additional Terms and Clues

2 Clues per Term

30 Unique Bingo Cards

Markers

1. **Either cut apart the book or make copies of ALL the sheets. You might want to make an extra copy of the clue sheets to use for introduction and review. Keep the sheets in an envelope for easy reuse.**

2. Cut apart the call cards with terms and clues.

3. Pass out one bingo card per student. There are enough for a class of 30.

4. Pass out markers. You may cut apart the markers included in this book or use any other small items of your choice.

5. Decide whether or not you will require the entire card to be filled. Requiring the entire card to be filled provides a better review. However, if you have a short time to fill, you may prefer to have them do the just the border or some other format. Tell the class before you begin what is required.

6. There are 50 terms. Read the list before you begin. If there are any terms that have not been covered in class, you may want to read to the students the term and clues before you begin.

7. There is a blank space in the middle of each card. You can instruct the students to use it as a free space or you can write in answers to cover terms not included. Of course, in this case you would create your own clues. (Templates provided.)

8. Shuffle the cards and place them in a pile. Two or three clues are provided for each term. If you plan to play the game with the same group more than once, you might want to choose a different clue for each game. If not, you may choose to use more than one clue.

9. Be sure to keep the cards you have used for the present game in a separate pile. When a student calls, "Bingo," he or she will have to verify that the correct answers are on his or her card AND that the markers were placed in response to the proper questions. Pull out the cards that are on the student's card keeping them in the order they were used in the game. Read each clue as it was given and ask the student to identify the correct answer from his or her card.

10. If the student has the correct answers on the card AND has shown that they were marked in response to the *correct questions,* then that student is the winner and the game is over. If the student does not have the correct answers on the card OR he or she marked the answers in response to *the wrong questions,* then the game continues until there is a proper winner.

11. If you want to play again, reshuffle the cards and begin again.

Have fun!

TERMS

abbreviation	noun
adjective	paragraph
adverb	past
antonym	period (.)
Apostrophe (')	plot
article	plural
author	prefix
capital letter	preposition
character	present
comma (,)	pronoun
conjunction	proper noun
consonant	punctuation
contraction	question mark (?)
compound word	quotation marks (" ")
-ed	rhyme
-er	root (word)
-es	-s
-est	setting
exclamation point (!)	singular
fiction	subject
future	suffix
homophones	syllables
-ing	synonym
interjection	verb
-ly	vowel(s)

Additional Terms

Choose as many terms as you would like and write them in the squares.
Repeat each as desired. Cut out the squares and randomly distribute them to the
class. Instruct the students to place the square on the center space of their card.

Clues for Additional Terms

Write two or three clues for each new term.

_____ 1. 2. 3.	_____ 1. 2. 3.
_____ 1. 2. 3.	_____ 1. 2. 3.
_____ 1. 2. 3.	_____ 1. 2. 3.

! ? . : , .	! ? . : , .	! ? . : , .	! ? . : , .	! ? . : , .
! ? . : , .	! ? . : , .	! ? . : , .	! ? . : , .	! ? . : , .
! ? . : , .	! ? . : , .	! ? . : , .	! ? . : , .	! ? . : , .
! ? . : , .	! ? . : , .	! ? . : , .	! ? . : , .	! ? . : , .
! ? . : , .	! ? . : , .	! ? . : , .	! ? . : , .	! ? . : , .
! ? . : , .	! ? . : , .	! ? . : , .	! ? . : , .	! ? . : , .
! ? . : , .	! ? . : , .	! ? . : , .	! ? . : , .	! ? . : , .

abbreviation	**adjective**
1. A shortened form of a word or word group.	1. This part of speech describes a noun.
2. Dr. is an ___ for the title "Doctor."	2. In the sentence "She is pretty," the word *pretty* is one.
3. Tsp. is an ___ for the word "teaspoon."	3. Some common ones are *big, small, smart, tall* and *short*.
adverb	**antonym**
1. This part of speech describes verbs and adjectives.	1. A word that has a meaning opposite to that of another word.
2. In the sentence "Walk slowly," the word *slowly* is one.	2. The word *big* is an ___ of the word *little*.
3. Some common ones are *quickly, happily, easily* and *very*.	2. The word *cold* is an ___ of the word *hot*.
Apostrophe (')	**article**
1. This mark is sometimes used to form a contraction.	1. This small set of words includes the words *a, an* and *the*.
2. This mark is used to show possession.	2. In the phrase the book, the ___ *the* refers to a particular book.
3. If we want to say that a book belongs to John, we add __s to John.	2. In the phrase a book, the ___ *a* does not refer to a particular book.
author	**capital letter**
1. A person who writes books, stories, or articles.	1. You should begin every sentence with one.
2. Dr. Seuss is the ___ of *The Cat in the Hat*.	2. When you write your name, it should begin with one.
2. Eric Carle is the ___ of *The Very Hungry Caterpillar*.	3. If you write the name of your state, it should begin with one.
character	**comma (,)**
1. The person whom a story is about is the main ___ of the story.	1. This punctuation mark is used to separate items in a series.
2. Alice is the main ___ in *Alice's Adventures in Wonderland*.	2. If you are writing today's date, put a ___ between the day and year.
3. Dorothy is the main ___ in *The Wizard of Oz*.	3. When writing our city and state, we put a ___ between them.

Language Arts Bingo

© Barbara M. Peller

conjunction	consonant
1. A ___ is a joining word. 2. Examples are the words *and, if, or* and *but.* 3. In the sentence "I ate pizza and salad," the word *and* is one.	1. A speech sound that is not a vowel. 2. The letters *b, c, d* and *f* are examples. 3. The letters a, *e, i , o* and *u* are the only letters never considered a ___.
contraction	**compound word**
1. The shortening of a word or word group. 2. The words *can't* and *don't* are examples. 3. An apostrophe replaces the missing letters in one.	1. A word with one or more stems. 2. An example of the type of word is *bookworm.* 3. An example of the type of word is *lighthouse.*
-ed	**-er**
1. This suffix is often added to a verb to change it to the past tense. 2. To change the verb *play* to the past tense add the suffix ___. 3. To change the verb *watch* to the past tense add the suffix ___.	1. This suffix is sometimes added to an adjective to compare 2 things. 2. If Jane gets better grades than Lisa, we might say that Jane is smart__. 3. If Bob is taller than Mike, we might say that Mike is short__.
-es	**-est**
1. We form the plural of some words by adding ___ instead of -s. 2. We add ___ to the word *beach* to make it plural. 3. If a word ends in *y,* we often change the *y* to *i* and add ___ to make it plural.	1. This suffix is sometimes added to an adjective to compare 3 or more things. 2. If Will is taller than Jim and Pat, we say that Will is the tall___. 3. If Sue is younger than Becca and Ann, we say that Sue is the young___.
exclamation point (!)	**fiction**
1. This mark is used to show strong emotion. 2. This mark is used with interjections, such as *wow* and *hurray.* 3. If you want to show surprise, you should end your sentence with one.	1. A story that is made up by the author. 2. Fantasy stories are ___ 3. Biographies are non-___.

Language Arts Bingo

future	homophones
1. This tense is a verb form that marks an event that did not yet happen.	1. They are pronounced the same but have different meanings.
2. "I will go to the store tomorrow" is an example of this tense.	2. *Hare* (the animal) and *hair* (on your head) are ___. So are pair (two) and pear (the fruit).
3. "I will do my homework later" is an example of this tense.	3. Sometimes they are called homonyms.

-ing	interjection
1. We can say "I go" or "I am go___."	1. We use this part of speech to show surprise or other emotion.
2. We can say "I like to read" or "I like read___."	2. In the following the word *wow* is one: "Wow! That's great."
3. We can say "I like to fish" or "I like fish___."	3. In the following the word *hurray* is one: "Hurray! We won the contest."

-ly	noun
1. We often use this suffix to change an adjective into an adverb.	1. This part of speech names a person, animal, place or thing.
2. To change the adjective *slow* to an adverb, we add this suffix.	2. A common ___ does not refer to a particular person, place or thing.
3. To change the adjective *quick* to an adverb, we add this suffix.	3. Examples of common nouns are *mother, father, country* and *river.*

paragraph	past
1. A group of closely related sentences.	1. This tense is a verb form that marks an event already happened.
2. A ___ should have a topic sentence.	2. "I went to the store yesterday" is an example of this tense.
3. You should indent at the beginning of each new one in a story.	3. "I finished my homework an hour ago" is an example of this tense.

period (.)	plot
1. This punctuation mark is used at the end of a declarative sentence.	1. The main story in a novel.
2. This punctuation mark at the end of a declarative sentence indicates a full stop.	2. The series of events in a story.
3. This punctuation mark is used with many abbreviations.	3. The arrangement of events in a story.

plural 1. We usually add an -s to a noun to form its ___ and show that there are more than one. 2. The ___ of *child* is *children.* 3. The ___ of *goose* is *geese.*	**prefix** 1. A group of letters attached to the beginning of a word. 2. The ___ -*im* makes a word negative. For example, *impossible* means "not possible." 3. The ___ *pre-* means "before."
preposition 1. A ___ is a position word. 2. Examples of this part of speech are by, *in, over, on,* and *near.* 3. In the following sentence the word *under* is one: "There is a mouse under the table."	**present** 1. This tense is a verb form that marks an event that is happening. 2. "I am eating dinner" is an example of this tense. 3. "I am washing the dishes" is an example of this tense.
pronoun 1. It is a word that takes the place of a noun. 2. In the sentence "She is reading a book" the word *she* is one. 3. In the sentence "Give the book to him" the word *him* is one.	**proper noun** 1. It is the name of a specific person, place or thing. 2. In the sentence "Jane is a popular girl" *Jane* is a ___ but *girl* is not. 3. This kind of word is capitalized no matter where it comes in a sentence.
punctuation 1. It is the use of marks and signs to separate words into units. 2. Three types of ___ marks are periods, commas, and question marks. 3. ___ clarifies the meaning of a sentence and separates structural units.	**question mark (?)** 1. We use this punctuation mark at the end of an interrogatory sentence. 2. If you ask a question, end the sentence with this. 3. A ___ belongs at the end of this sentence: Who wants dessert__
quotation marks (" ") 1. These punctuation marks are used to set off spoken language. 2. ___ sometimes set off titles of things such as short stories and poems 3. ___ belong before the word *Here* and after the comma: _Here it is,_ she said.	**rhyme** 1. To be similar in sound, especially the endings of words. 2. The words *book* and *look* ___ 3. The words *car* and *far* ___

Language Arts Bingo

root (word)	**-s**
1. The form of a word after all prefixes and suffixes are removed.	1. Most words form a plural by adding this suffix or the suffix -es.
2. This part of the word contains its basic meaning.	2. To form the plural of the word *sock* add this suffix.
3. Another term for this is *stem.*	3. To form the plural of the word *book* add this suffix.
setting	**singular**
1. The time and place where something happens.	1. Denoting only one person, place or thing.
2. It describes where and when a story takes place.	2. The word *book* is ___; the word *books* is plural.
3. Castles are the ___ for many fairy tales.	3. The word *desk* is ___; the word *desks* is plural.
subject	**suffix**
1. The part of the sentence that tells what it is about.	1. A group of letters attached to the end of a word.
2. The ___ of "The girl is doing her homework" is "The girl."	2. The ___ -*ness* means "state of being." *Happiness* means "the state of being happy."
3. The ___ of "Jenny is eating ice cream" is "Jenny."	3. The ___ -*less* means "without."
syllables	**synonym**
1. Units of spoken language bigger than a phoneme (the smallest unit).	1. A word having the same or almost the same meaning of another.
2. There are 2 ___ in the word *reading.*	2. *Frigid* is a ___ for *cold.*
3. There are 3 ___ in the word *magazine.*	3. *Large* is a ___ for *big.*
verb	**vowel(s)**
1. It is a doing or action word.	1. *a, e, i o,* or *u.*
2. The following are examples: *go, eat, walk, sit, read,* and *write.*	2. Sometimes the letter *y* is a consonant and sometimes it is a ___.
3. In the sentence "She reads a book every night" the word *reads* is one.	3. There are 2 ___ in the word *setting: e* and *i.*

Language Arts Bingo

© **Barbara M. Peller**

Language Arts Bingo

-ing	Exclamation Point (!)	Singular	Verb	Suffix
Capital Letter	Abbreviation	Synonym	Plot	Homophones
Rhyme	Punctuation		-ly	Plural
Vowel(s)	Present	-es	-s	Interjection
Pronoun	Consonant	Character	-er	-est

Language Arts Bingo

Vowel(s)	Setting	Paragraph	Prefix	Pronoun
Interjection	Plot	Adjective	Present	Quotation Marks (" ")
Proper Noun	Consonant		Comma (,)	-es
-ed	Root (Word)	Punctuation	Noun	Homophones
-est	Synonym	Character	Capital Letter	-er

Language Arts Bingo

Vowel(s)	-es	Plot	-s	Rhyme
Consonant	Abbreviation	Article	Exclamation Point (!)	Future
Present	Synonym		Quotation Marks (" ")	Adverb
Punctuation	Proper Noun	Pronoun	-ed	Paragraph
-er	Capital Letter	Character	Noun	Singular

Language Arts Bingo

Punctuation	Quotation Marks (" ")	Pronoun	Capital Letter	Singular
Past	Adjective	Exclamation Point (!)	Prefix	Rhyme
-ly	-ed		Suffix	Verb
-es	Question Mark (?)	Synonym	Character	Article
Fiction	-est	Period (.)	-er	Plural

Language Arts Bingo

-est	Suffix	Present	Adjective	Capital Letter
Past	-es	Article	Comma (,)	Abbreviation
Setting	Plural		Conjunction	Contraction
Homophones	Quotation Marks (" ")	-ing	Noun	Fiction
Plot	Character	Question Mark (?)	Punctuation	-ly

Language Arts Bingo: Card No. 5

Language Arts Bingo

Adverb	Quotation Marks (" ")	Paragraph	Setting	Plural
-s	Present	Fiction	Exclamation Point (!)	Rhyme
Prefix	Article		Adjective	Comma (,)
Character	Pronoun	Noun	Period (.)	Singular
Interjection	-es	-ing	-ly	Question Mark (?)

Language Arts Bingo

-ing	Quotation Marks (" ")	Contraction	Conjunction	Plot
Interjection	Singular	Consonant	Abbreviation	Past
Paragraph	Verb		Comma (,)	Antonym
Punctuation	-ed	Apostrophe (')	Vowel(s)	Proper Noun
Character	Capital Letter	Noun	Period (.)	Adverb

Language Arts Bingo

-ly	Quotation Marks (" ")	Author	-s	Antonym
Past	Setting	Prefix	Plural	Adjective
Rhyme	Preposition		Singular	Suffix
-er	Punctuation	Vowel(s)	Fiction	-ed
Synonym	Character	Period (.)	Present	Interjection

Language Arts Bingo

Comma (,)	Plot	Consonant	Rhyme	Plural
Fiction	Setting	-ly	Present	Singular
Future	-ing		Abbreviation	Author
Apostrophe (')	-est	Pronoun	Conjunction	Contraction
-ed	Noun	Article	Vowel(s)	Suffix

Language Arts Bingo: Card No. 9

Language Arts Bingo

Vowel(s)	-s	Adjective	Prefix	Question Mark (?)
Plural	Antonym	Exclamation Point (!)	Abbreviation	Singular
Preposition	Quotation Marks (" ")		Verb	Proper Noun
Pronoun	Homophones	Fiction	Noun	Future
Apostrophe (')	Interjection	Paragraph	-est	-ly

Language Arts Bingo: Card No. 10

Language Arts Bingo

Adverb	Quotation Marks (" ")	Present	Fiction	Interjection
Author	Future	Conjunction	Comma (,)	Exclamation Point (!)
Past	Setting		Paragraph	Consonant
Apostrophe (')	Rhyme	Noun	Capital Letter	Vowel(s)
Article	Character	-ing	Period (.)	Plot

© Barbara M. Peller

Language Arts Bingo

Plot	Suffix	Future	-s	Comma (,)
Consonant	Synonym	Setting	Period (.)	Abbreviation
-ing	Contraction		Plural	Prefix
Character	-ed	Singular	Vowel(s)	Past
Quotation Marks (" ")	Author	Preposition	Article	Antonym

Language Arts Bingo

Apostrophe (')	Suffix	Adverb	Future	Plural
Setting	Author	Quotation Marks (" ")	Comma (,)	Proper Noun
-s	Adjective		Consonant	Contraction
-ly	Noun	Antonym	Preposition	Vowel(s)
Character	Homophones	Period (.)	-ing	Conjunction

Language Arts Bingo

Capital Letter	Setting	Present	Comma (,)	Apostrophe (')
Antonym	-ing	Future	Abbreviation	Quotation Marks (" ")
Fiction	Verb		Paragraph	Article
Homophones	Noun	Preposition	Adjective	Adverb
Character	Prefix	Proper Noun	Interjection	-ly

Language Arts Bingo

Conjunction	Comma (,)	Present	Plot	-s
Adverb	Paragraph	Exclamation Point (!)	Setting	Fiction
Plural	-ing		Rhyme	Singular
Character	Future	Author	Noun	Apostrophe (')
Interjection	-ed	Period (.)	Question Mark (?)	Consonant

Language Arts Bingo

Adjective	Future	Author	Question Mark (?)	Root (Word)
Prefix	Proper Noun	Contraction	Past	Verb
Apostrophe (')	Suffix		Plural	Consonant
Punctuation	Antonym	Character	Conjunction	Vowel(s)
Fiction	Syllables	Period (.)	-ed	Quotation Marks (" ")

Language Arts Bingo: Card No. 16

Language Arts Bingo

Apostrophe (')	Subject	Compound Word	Future	Capital Letter
Conjunction	Fiction	Noun	Verb	Contraction
Comma (,)	-ly		Syllables	Author
-est	Interjection	Vowel(s)	Present	Proper Noun
Pronoun	Article	Plot	-s	Suffix

© Barbara M. Peller

Language Arts Bingo

Question Mark (?)	Preposition	Antonym	Fiction	Prefix
Quotation Marks (" ")	Apostrophe (')	Pronoun	Plural	Article
Comma (,)	Proper Noun		Compound Word	Singular
-est	Exclamation Point (!)	Noun	Vowel(s)	Paragraph
Syllables	Future	Present	Subject	Adverb

Language Arts Bingo

Plural	Adverb	Future	Author	Preposition
Conjunction	-s	Singular	Plot	Verb
Subject	Capital Letter		Abbreviation	Question Mark (?)
Paragraph	Syllables	Pronoun	-ed	Compound Word
Rhyme	Root (Word)	Interjection	-ly	Period (.)

Language Arts Bingo

Preposition	Subject	-s	Future	Abbreviation
Adjective	Consonant	Past	Pronoun	Prefix
Suffix	Contraction		Punctuation	Exclamation Point (!)
-est	Synonym	-er	-ed	Syllables
-es	-ly	Root (Word)	Vowel(s)	Compound Word

Language Arts Bingo

Conjunction	Adverb	Past	Future	Homophones
Suffix	Compound Word	Antonym	Author	-ing
Proper Noun	Interjection		Subject	Present
Pronoun	Plot	Syllables	-est	-ly
Punctuation	Root (Word)	Period (.)	Apostrophe (')	-ed

Language Arts Bingo

Rhyme	Paragraph	Compound Word	Setting	Apostrophe (')
Prefix	-s	Question Mark (?)	Author	Abbreviation
Antonym	Verb		-ing	Contraction
Syllables	-est	-ed	Exclamation Point (!)	Capital Letter
Root (Word)	Article	Subject	Proper Noun	Past

Language Arts Bingo

Adjective	Subject	Plot	Setting	Period (.)
Adverb	Preposition	Interjection	Conjunction	Exclamation Point (!)
Paragraph	Apostrophe (')		-er	-ing
Proper Noun	Root (Word)	Syllables	Article	-ed
Homophones	Synonym	-ly	Pronoun	Compound Word

Language Arts Bingo

Adjective	Preposition	Capital Letter	Subject	Author
Plural	Period (.)	Past	Prefix	-ing
Contraction	Question Mark (?)		Apostrophe (')	Proper Noun
Homophones	-er	Syllables	Article	Suffix
-es	Punctuation	Root (Word)	-s	Synonym

Language Arts Bingo

Punctuation	Past	Subject	Present	Compound Word
Exclamation Point (!)	Homophones	Conjunction	Antonym	Abbreviation
Suffix	Author		-er	Syllables
Question Mark (?)	-est	Synonym	Root (Word)	Verb
Period (.)	Capital Letter	Paragraph	Fiction	-es

Language Arts Bingo

Compound Word	Subject	Paragraph	Prefix	Question Mark (?)
Pronoun	-s	Author	Preposition	Adjective
Homophones	-er		Verb	Punctuation
Apostrophe (')	Setting	-est	Root (Word)	Syllables
Contraction	Fiction	Present	Synonym	-es

Language Arts Bingo

Paragraph	Antonym	Subject	Preposition	Consonant
Homophones	-er	Conjunction	Syllables	Abbreviation
Noun	Synonym		Root (Word)	Punctuation
Question Mark (?)	Adverb	Past	-es	Exclamation Point (!)
Apostrophe (')	Verb	Compound Word	Rhyme	Contraction

Language Arts Bingo

Plural	Preposition	Question Mark (?)	Subject	Antonym
Consonant	Compound Word	-er	Prefix	Verb
Synonym	Proper Noun		Contraction	Pronoun
Vowel(s)	Rhyme	Interjection	Root (Word)	Syllables
Setting	Comma (,)	Apostrophe (')	-es	Homophones

Language Arts Bingo

Compound Word	Preposition	Question Mark (?)	Conjunction	Comma (,)
Homophones	Pronoun	Past	Contraction	Rhyme
Suffix	-er		Abbreviation	Subject
Consonant	-est	Singular	Root (Word)	Syllables
Adjective	Author	-es	Adverb	Synonym

Language Arts Bingo: Card No. 29

Language Arts Bingo

Capital Letter	Subject	Prefix	Comma (,)	Syllables
Exclamation Point (!)	Preposition	Paragraph	Verb	Abbreviation
Homophones	Apostrophe (')		Contraction	Past
-es	Adverb	Singular	Root (Word)	-er
-est	Plot	Synonym	Compound Word	Question Mark (?)

www.ingramcontent.com/pod-product-compliance
Lightning Source LLC
LaVergne TN
LVHW061341060426
835511LV00014B/2051